The mathematical disco

WHO IS THE BEST FORMULA 1 DRIVER OF ALL TIME

Jaren Cowan

All rights reserved 2021

Any form of reproduction of this work, in whole or in part, without the express consent of its author, in any graphic, electronic or mechanical means, including photocopying or recording or any other information retrieval and storage system, is prohibited.

Cover graphic resources: wikiwand.com / 24sata.hr

INTRODUCTION

Who is the best Formula 1 driver of all time? This is a question that has generated thousands of discussions. "Senna! Nobody piloted like him! If I hadn't had that accident... ". "The best driver was Fangio, he won with any car!"

There are many possible answers ... and the truth is that it is difficult to establish which is the true one. It is an impossible question with a complex answer to determine. Cars have changed over time. The machine is becoming more and more important. The way of competing is different, and so are the opportunities.

Today it is even almost impossible to determine who is the best driver on the grid. Is Hamilton the best driver today? Could any other driver surpass him if he also had a car as advantageous as the Mercedes?

If it is already difficult to guess who is the best driver today, imagine trying to do it in a line through time, where the competition conditions have been so changing, as well as the regulations, the vehicles, the circuits ...

However, in this book we are going to dare to answer that question, and for this we will assess every aspect that influences the quality of a pilot. We will compare the best drivers in history in those points of interest that are decisive in the car race of these heroes. We will score them on each of those relevant factors, so that we can make them "compete" with each other.

We will focus, by popular acclaim, on thirteen of the big names on everyone's lips when it comes to tackling this issue. Surely many who deserve it will be left out of this Top 13, but we will all agree that the best driver of all time is among them.

If this analysis is of interest, as I hope, in the future we could extend it to those great drivers who are left out in this test. The results could be very interesting.

So, without further delay and since speed is what determines these heroes of the asphalt the most, let's proceed to try to compare, as far as possible, these talented drivers who appear in everyone's head when trying to solve the difficult question of who is the best Formula 1 driver of all time.

CHILDHOOD AND ADOLESCENCE

The first factor that we are going to analyze to begin this analysis is the first stage of the life of the pilots. Although by then they were still far from becoming the heroes that they would become, although they were just beginning to dream of sitting in a car to become champions, childhood is a factor to take into account to define how talented a driver is.

Today, future drivers are practically born on top of a car. As soon as they have the ability to drive, their parents (if they have the opportunity) put them as soon as possible in a vehicle adapted to their age. It is not uncommon today to find children under the age of ten competing in kart races.

That facilitates learning and development. The earlier a person begins to compete, the more he will develop his abilities. However, pilots from earlier times did not have these opportunities. In the first decades of the championship, it was normal for drivers to start participating in Formula 1 beyond 30 years, even 40.

In these cases, they were absolutely dependent on their natural talent. They hadn't had years and years of prior apprenticeship to hone and improve their abilities. That is, the later you start driving, the more important your natural driving skills become.

Therefore, we could affirm that a pilot who starts racing later and becomes champion has a more developed natural talent than one who has developed his abilities through continuous learning and practice.

And that is what we are going to discover in this first section.

JUAN MANUEL FANGIO

Juan Manuel Fangio was born in Balcarce (Argentina) on June 24, 1911. He was the fourth child of a couple of Italian immigrants. As a child he was best known for another sport, soccer. For this reason, he was known as "el croco" for his talent when it came to scoring goals with his left foot in games with his friends.

Es.wikipedia.org

At age 9 he began working to help his family financially in a smithy. At the age of 11 he began his relationship with vehicles, going to work at the Rugby dealership. There he began to drive thanks to his mentor Raimundo Carlini, and Fangio describes those first experiences as if he could feel the life of the vehicles he was driving.

Two years later he would go to work for Ford, where he would obtain a great learning about mechanics, more specifically at the engine level. At age 16, he would buy his first car, an Overland (Jeep).

After overcoming pleurisy that had him resting for almost a year, Fangio developed in football and boxing.

However, he would not abandon his fixation for motorsports, accompanying Manuel Ayerza in a zonal competition in which he would finish second with a Chevrolet. He also accompanied his brother-in-law José Brujas Font, but pneumonia would force him to stop working for two months.

Later it would be the military service that would take him away from all sports.

On his return in 1932 and at the age of twenty-one, he created a mechanical workshop with a friend thanks to land contributed by his father and a truck donated by footballer Francisco Cavalloti. It was during his time in this workshop that he finally began to be part of the automobile competition.

Conclution: As we will see later, 21 years is a very late age to compete. Although he would have the automobile facilities of working in a workshop, Fangio also did not have much financial aid or resources related to regulated competitions to get started in motorsports. Therefore, a score of 8/10 would be appropriate in this section.

STIRLING MOSS

Stirling Moss was born in London on September 17, 1929. His parents were already familiar with motorsport. His father had come to compete in the 1924 Indianapolis 500, obtaining 16th place. His mother had also been actively involved in piloting a Singer Nine before the war.

Stirling studied in several schools where he suffered harassment due to his Jewish origins, but far from victimizing himself he used it as a motivation to continually improve himself and prove his worth. At age nine, his father gave him an Austin 7 where he began driving through the countryside. Four years later, he would buy his first car once he obtained his driver's license. Due to nephritis, he was spared military service.

His automobile career began in 1948 with his father's BMW 328. He made his competition debut at the age of 19, two before Fangio.

Conclution:Moss also began competing at a later age, although with more ease because his parents were already familiar with competition. Your score in this case is 6/10.

Metro.co.uk

JIM CLARK

Jim Clark was born on March 4, 1936, on a farm in Fife, Scotland. Being the youngest of five siblings, as was tradition, he had the duty to take care of the family farm, which made it difficult for him to enter motoring.

However, despite family opposition, he managed to start competing in local rally events, debuting with his own Sunbeam-Talbot. It therefore began to develop in local rallies at the age of 20, a similar age and at the same time intermediate between Moss and Fangio.

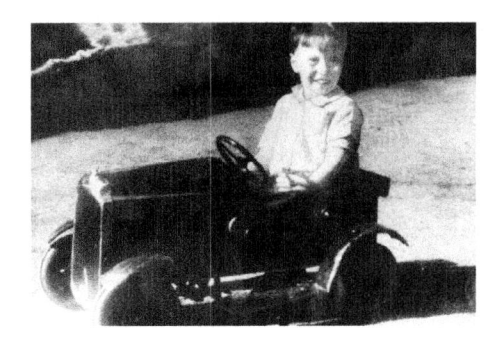

Pinterest.com

Conclution: With a starting age similar to the previous ones but also with a humble origin and difficulty in obtaining resources, his score is 8/10.

JACKIE STEWART

Sir John Young Stewart was born on June 11, 1939 in Milton, Scotland. He was born into a family that was fond of the motor world, so he was quickly drawn to racing. His parents sold Jaguar cars in a store, which facilitated his access to the automotive world. In the garage he was able to learn a lot about mechanics.

He also had the reference of his brother Jimmy, who was a well-known local pilot.

Stewart, due to his dyslexia, did not receive high academic accolades, which is why he decided to focus even more on motorsport. He spent his first years from workshop to workshop, immersed in the motor world, combining it with his talent for clay pigeon shooting, where he had options to compete in the 1960 Olympic Games, although he finally finished third in the British team.

The first vehicle Stewart bought was an Austin A30. In 1961, Barry Filer, who was a client of the family business, loaned him several cars with which he began to compete, such as a Marcos and an Aston Martin DB4. Therefore, at 22 years old and similar in age to the previous pilots, although with more family facilities, Stewart was already launching himself into the world of competition.

Conclusion: Following the previous scales, due to his late age when starting in the competition but due to his economic facilities and growing up in an environment familiar with cars, his score is 6/10.

Worthpoint.com

EMERSON FITTIPALDI

Fittipaldi was born on December 12, 1946 in Sao Paulo, Brazil. His father, Wilson Fittipaldi, was a famous radio commentator and his mother Józefa Wojciechowska a Russian immigrant.

His father was related to the motor world by driving cars after World War II. This made both Emerson and his brother Wilson fond of motorsports.

Thus, Emerson became a motorcycle racer at the young age of 14 and two years later he was already piloting seaplanes. A seaplane accident by his brother caused him to focus more on competitions on land. In 1967 he was already competing and winning the 6 hours of Interlagos with a Volkswagen Karmann Ghia. Therefore, after his 20 years it can be said that Fittipaldi was already competing more than effectively.

Conclution: with a late age to compete and with a parent slightly familiar with motor vehicles, his score is 7/10.

Pinterest.es

NIKI LAUDA

Andreas Nikolaus Lauda was born on February 22, 1949 in Vienna, Austria. He did it in the bosom of a wealthy family thanks to the paper industry.

Ro.pinterest.com

His family fervently opposed his passion for motorsports, but despite such opposition they could not prevent him from racing a Mini. His talent was such that before he reached the age of 20 he was already racing private sports cars from the Porsche and Chevron brands.

Conclution: Following the previous reasoning, a late age to start competing together with a greater availability of resources give it a score of 7/10 in this section.

NIGEL MANSELL

Nigel Mansell was born on August 8, 1953 in Worcestershire, United Kingdom. The son of an engineer, he also did not have family support and had to face disapproval from his parents in order to gain a foothold in motorsport.

Reddit.com

Despite this, it managed to make a niche for itself in kart competitions, at a time when these vehicles were beginning to be used as the starting point of the automobile race and beginning to make use of a process that would become normalized throughout. weather.

In 1976, at 23 years of age, he already made a niche for himself in Formula Ford, establishing the beginnings of his sports career, although it would take a long time to reach success.

Conclution: Mansell was one of those who would start competing later, which together with disapproval and little family support give him a score of 9/10.

ALAIN PROST

Alain Marie Pascal Prost was born on February 24, 1955 in Lorette, France. Despite his short stature (1.67 m), he was a child who was very participative in various sports disciplines such as soccer, skating or wrestling.

Pinterest.es

Although he valued dedicating himself professionally to some of these sports, it was at the age of 14 when he started driving karts that he realized that his future was in motorsport. It can be said, therefore, that Prost took control of a vehicle and competed at a much younger age than his predecessors.

Conclution: At age 14, Prost began competing at an intermediate age, giving him a score of 5/10.

AYRTON SENNA

Ayrton Senna da Silva, born in Sao Paulo on March 21, 1960, belonged to a wealthy family, owners of the Milton da Silva factory. Senna showed athletic skills from a very young age and at the young age of 4 he already had a fondness for motorsports and cars.

Grandprixhistory.org

Up to three years, he had shown coordination problems, however medical tests would not find any problems. Thus, with only 7 years, Senna learned to drive on the family farm on the edge of a Jeep.

His first go-kart was home-built with a lawnmower motor, but this led him to compete at the young age of 13 at Interlagos, in a test that he led for much of the time even though he would end up colliding with a partner.

Conclution: With a similar age to that of Prost to start in the competition but with more economic resources to do it in better conditions, his score is 4/10.

MICHAEL SCHUMACHER

Michael Schumacher was born on January 3, 1969 in Hürth, West Germany, the son of a bricklayer. At the age of four, his father Rolf Schumacher transformed his toy pedal kart by adding a motorcycle engine. Michael would end up colliding with a lamp post.

Pinterest.cl

Despite this, Michael would eventually join the Kerpen-Horrem karting club, becoming its youngest member. His father, from individual pieces, managed to build him a competitive kart with which, at just 6 years old, he won the first club championship. A very premature talent, which began to develop from a very young age.

Conclution: with a great precocity when starting to compete and therefore have more options to learn early, his score in this section is reduced to 2/10.

FERNANDO ALONSO

Fernando Alonso Díaz was born in Oviedo, Asturias, on July 29, 1981. His father, José Luis Alonso, was an amateur kart driver, which led him to build a kart for his daughter Lorena to share his hobby. She was not interested because it was her brother Fernando who took advantage of the vehicle, obtaining a karting license at the young age of five.

Mhcarsculture.blogspot.com

For his stage in karting, his entire family, from humble origins, turned to support him. His father acted as a mechanic and representative while his mother made the competition suits for him. They also ensured that Fernando enjoyed a good academic position. In this way, at age 7, he managed to win his first karting race.

Conclution: in this case we find ourselves with an age similar to that of the kaiser, so again the score is 2/10.

SEBASTIAN VETTEL

Sebastian Vettel was born on July 3, 1987 in Heppenheim, Germany. Although he confesses that he would have liked to be a singer, the truth is that his life in motorsport began very early. With only three years he was already driving karts and at 8 years old he was already participating in competitions.

Conclution: Vettel took very little longer to start racing than the previous two, so the score is 3/10.

Reddit.com

LEWIS HAMILTON

Lewis Carl Davidson Hamilton was born on January 7, 1985 in Stevenage, England. With only two years he had to face the separation of his parents, going to live alternately with one and the other.

Grandprixhistory.org

His first experience in motor racing was curiously with radio-controlled remote-controlled cars. His father bought him a remote control car at the age of five with which he competed in the BRCA national championship.

At the age of six, his father would buy him a kart and he would become his main supporter, constantly changing jobs to be able to support and provide his son with everything he needed to compete. Thus, at the age of eight Hamilton began to compete in karting where he showed rapid progress.

Conclution: similar to Vettel in age of onset, his score is 3/10.

PROVISIONAL CLASSIFICATION

Mansell	9
Fangio	8
Clark	8
Lauda	7
Fittipaldi	7
Stewart	6
Moss	6
Prost	5
Senna	4
Hamilton	3
Vettel	3
Alonso	2
Schumacher	2

TIME OF ARRIVAL AT F1

In this second section we are going to analyze the time it took each driver to get to Formula 1 since he started racing. We are going to emphasize that first stage as drivers.

The more talented a driver shows early in his career, the more sponsorships and more and better teams look to him to take advantage of his driving skills.

It can therefore be deduced that, apart from the luck factor and the circumstances of the time of each of the pilots, the higher the quality, the shorter the time required to reach the maximum competition.

Great drivers are hunted by great teams. They develop more easily and quickly in the different categories to advance through them until they reach the maximum automobile competition in the world.

So let's see how they progressed from their first racing adventure and rate that development until they finally managed to get a seat in the fastest cars in the universe.

JUAN MANUEL FANGIO

Fangio began competing in local races in 1936 with a Ford Model A that he himself had repaired and rebuilt in his own workshop. He prospered and four years later he became the National Champion of Argentina, a feat that he repeated in 1941.

It should be borne in mind that these competitions were far from Formula 1 (which did not yet have an official championship) and instead of on closed circuits, they competed over long distances such as the 10,000-kilometer Northern Grand Prix over 15 days.

His success was increasing, collecting victories in important races such as "Mar y sierra" until the Second World War paralyzed the world. Finished the warlike fight, returned to compete and to add victories.

In 1948, a tragic accident that led to the death of his co-driver Daniel Urrutia, leading him to depression, was about to take him away from the competition. Fangio managed to recover from the trance and returned to the path of victory to the point that the Argentine Automobile Club bought him a Maserati so that he could compete in Europe.

When the first Formula 1 World Championship was organized in 1950, Fangio was already so prestigious that the Alfa Romeo team hired him with Luigi Fagioli and Giuseppe Farina.

Motorpasion.com

This means that, for the first edition of the Formula 1 championship, Juan Manuel Fangio was one of the few chosen that would be part of this first season. Or what is the same, he was considered one of the most talented drivers when the championship was created.

Conclution:Fangio participated in Formula 1 in the first attempt in which it was possible, that is, when the championship was created. This cannot leave a rating other than 10/10.

STIRLING MOSS

Moss began racing his father's BMW 328, and the proceeds from it were used to purchase a Cooper 500 in 1948. This allowed him to excel in national and later international races, reaching Formula 3.

In 1950, the year of the creation of the Formula 1 World Championship, Moss enjoyed his victories in the rally discipline. In 1951 he had an offer from Enzo Ferrari to compete in Formula 2 that did not materialize, since his position would be filled by Piero Taruffi. However, he would get a niche in Formula 1 at the 1951 Swiss Grand Prix aboard an HWM.

Statsf1.com

Conclution: Moss would take a little longer than Fangio to participate in Formula 1 and would also have to do so largely for his own worth as he did not have the confidence of official teams (until 1953 he would compete with an official Cooper). Therefore, having a more blocked arrival to F1, his score is 6/10.

JIM CLARK

In 1958, two years after starting in motorsport, Clark was already part of the local Border Rivers team, where with a Jaguar D-Type and a Porsche he would achieve 18 national victories.

In 1959 he would get tenth place at Le Mans with a Lotus Elite, a performance that would make Colin Chapman want to have him for his Formula Junior team. In 1960, Jim Clark won the first race of the category in a Lotus Ford.

His performance earned him a place in Lotus in the Dutch Formula 1 Grand Prix of the same year to replace Surtees.

Noticias.coches.com

Conclution: Clark seized every opportunity, moving up quickly and was always on target for different teams, progress that gives him a score of 8/10.

JACKIE STEWART

In 1961, Barry Filer, a client of his family's company, provided him with a Marcos to compete with which he achieved four victories. In 1962 he would pilot a Jaguar E-Type where he would obtain two more local victories. The victories would continue to increase in 1963 and 1964.

By then, Ken Tyrrell became interested in his evolution and granted him a test for the Cooper Car Company Formula Junior team. Stewart did the test with a McLaren Formula 3 with which he shone, achieving the best times of the car. This earned him a spot on the team.

His Formula 3 debut at Snetterton was brilliant, 25 seconds ahead of the runner-up. He was offered a test in Formula 1, but Stewart preferred to continue to gain experience in Tyrrell's team, where he became the F3 champion.

Stewart did a Formula 1 test for Lotus with which he astonished Colin Chapman and Jim Clark, but again he preferred to be cautious and compete in Formula 2.

In 1965 his first opportunity in Formula 1 would come at Lotus to replace Jim Clark, who was injured. In his first Formula 1 race at the Rand Grand Prix he took pole, and although the car suffered a breakdown in the first race, he won the second and set the fastest lap.

Pinterest.com

Conclution: Stewart's rise to Formula 1 was brilliant, since its origins in competition he had always been interested in offering him cars and took every opportunity to move up the category. Only his caution leaves his score at 8/10.

EMERSON FITTIPALDI

At the age of 20, Fittipaldi already achieved his first triumphs, highlighting the victory of the 6 Hours of Interlagos with a Volkswagen Karmann Ghia. The following year he would also get victory in the 12 Hours of Porto Alegre.

Together with his brother, they went on to compete in Formula Vee, a more open and lower-cost motorsport competition that gave them the possibility to compete. At the age of 21, he was already proclaimed champion of this competition, thus showing his talent.

The following year he traveled to Europe looking for greater possibilities, increasing his successes in Formula Ford, which would lead him to sign for Jim Russell for Formula 3. With the Lotus 59 he would win nine races to finish champion that same season.

The following year in 1970 Fittipaldi promoted to Formula 2 with the Lotus Bardahl team, and although he would not get the championship, his regularity in the first positions would make him be third classified. However, he already had his sights set on Formula 1.

The Lotus Formula 1 team decided to use their third car to test young talents. As of July 1970, Fittipaldi began to occupy this third seat, highlighting his fourth position in Germany.

After the death of Jochen Rindt at Monza and the departure of John Miles, Lotus was left without its main drivers, leaving Fittipaldi as the team's starting driver. The Brazilian seized the opportunity and won his first race in the United States, fulfilling the trust placed in him.

Pinterest.com

Conclution: Fitipaldi seized one opportunity after another. Although in the beginning he had to find the means to compete in Formula Vee, he soon became the goal of many teams and took advantage of his trip to Europe in which he gave himself 3 months to succeed. He finally got the opportunity in Formula 1 in a quality team, which gives him a score of 8/10, not being higher for not having managed to win Formula 2.

NIKI LAUDA

Lauda also sought his opportunity in Formula Vee after having successfully raced in a Mini. He also drove for private brands such as Porsche and Chevron, however, feeling that his progress was stagnating, he opted to request a bank loan to buy a position in the March team in Formula 2.

Due to his talent that impressed March's director, Robin Herd, in 1972 he alternated races in the team between Formula 1 and Formula 2. However, the team did not obtain the expected performance and after a season of poor results, Lauda decided to take out another loan to get a seat on the BRM team.

Statsf1.com

Conclution: Despite Niki Lauda's undoubted talent, he had to actively seek his seat and put in money to secure his chances, and he was also not fortunate that the big teams required his participation, lowering his score in this regard to 4/10.

NIGEL MANSELL

Mansell, despite his late start in the competition, opted for what would end up becoming the most common method of entering motorsport: karting. His successes with karts led him to compete in Formula Ford, where in 1976 he made his debut with victory in his first race, finishing the year with a total of 9 wins.

The following year he won 33 races of the 42 that he participated in Formula Ford to get proclaimed champion of the category. This season he had an accident that nearly cost him bodily paralysis from a neck injury. Doctors recommended that he not drive again, but he requested discharge to continue the season.

Between 1978 and 1980 Mansell competed in Formula 3. After a first year with a vehicle that was not very competitive, he signed for David Price Racing, with whom he would finish eighth. Again he would suffer an accident that would damage his vertebrae.

Despite the body pain, he accepted a Colin Chapman test for Lotus along with other drivers with the aim of getting the second seat of the team in Formula 1. Mansell did not get the position to accompany Mario Andretti, but he did get a position as a driver tester on the computer.

His good performance as a test driver gave him the opportunity to make his Formula 1 debut at the Austrian Grand Prix in 1980. He was not very lucky in his debut, with a fuel leak that caused burns on his buttocks and with engine failures that forced him to withdraw in his first two participations. But his insistence had served to gain a foothold in Formula 1.

Topgear.es

Conclution: Mansell took more time to move up from category to category, but there was always interest in him from the teams, which, together with his insistence and his ability to overcome, gave him a score of 6/10 in this category.

ALAIN PROST

Prost also got his start in karting, as the vast majority of drivers in the modern era would end up doing. After several successes in the category, he decided to leave his studies at the age of 19 to dedicate himself completely to motorsport. By working as a go-kart mechanic, he was able to finance himself.

In 1975 he was proclaimed champion of the senior karting championship in France, which earned him a year's prize in Formula Renault. In the season that he debuted in French Formula Renault, he won all but one race.

The following year, he would win Formula Renault champion again, this time European, which would earn him a place in Formula 3. Once again, he would repeat French and European triumphs in this new category. By then, having been named champion of each category in which he debuted, he already had offers from several Formula 1 teams. Finally, he would agree to sign for McLaren.

Although he received an offer to participate as a third driver in the last Grand Prix of 1979, Prost decided to dispense with a one-time participation to focus on the 1980 season, where he would begin his career in F1.

F1.fansite.com

Conclution: Since his rise to Formula Renault, Prost has only become champion of each new category in which he participated, and would jump from Formula 3 to Formula 1 with several offers on the table. Nothing to blame on a practically perfect path to the top category: 10/10.

AYRTON SENNA

Senna also started in the world of karting, winning the South American championship in 1977. Later, he would end up participating in the world karting championship for five consecutive years, being runner-up twice.

Like many other South American drivers, he would have to travel to Europe to progress and in 1981 he traveled to England to start racing in single-seaters, winning the Formula Ford 1600 with the Van Diemen team.

Despite the success, Senna announced her retirement to contribute to the family business. However, an offer to compete in Formula Ford 2000 in 1982 together with the arrival of several sponsorships gave him the opportunity to continue, proclaiming himself champion of both the British and European categories.

In 1983 he made the leap to Formula 3 with the West Surrey Racing team. Senna dominated the first part of the championship while Martin Brundle did so in the second part. Finally, in an exciting final race, the Brazilian managed to clinch the title.

That same year he became a test driver for a wide variety of Formula 1 teams: McLaren, Williams, Brabham and Lotus. In 1984 he continued as a test driver for Lotus, McLaren and Brabham, but with contracts with more expectations of getting to compete in the near future.

Senna was very demanding when it came to receiving a very personalized treatment to get a car as adapted to him as possible, which made his jump to Formula 1 difficult.

Added to that was the difficulty of his nationality. While McLaren and Brabham were willing to accept their terms, knowing Senna's great talent, the sponsors of these teams wanted a British driver for McLaren and an Italian driver for Brabham.

Senna had no choice but to accept the offer of Toleman, a new team and less competitive than the previous ones. At least, that way he managed to gain a foothold in the top competition.

Grandprix247.com

Conclution:Senna's rise to F1 was somewhat hampered. Although he did not clearly stand out with titles in karting and had to cross the Atlantic to Europe to take off, his time in Formula Ford and Formula 3 was impeccable, to delay his jump to F1 again after a long time as a driver. of tests to finish in one of the weakest teams on the grid. That uneven progress gives him a score of 6/10.

MICHAEL SCHUMACHER

After his victory at just 6 years old in a karting club championship, his parents went out of their way to provide everything he needed to keep racing. However, the cost was excessive and unaffordable, but thanks to the support of local entrepreneurs, little Schumacher was able to continue progressing.

In 1982 at the age of 13, he won the German Junior Kart Championship. He had to do it with a Luxembourg license, since in Germany the karting license could only be obtained from 14 years old. Until 1988, he managed to become champion of countless German and European championships.

So much talent on board a kart would give him the opportunity to compete in Formula 3 in the WTS team. He won the German series in 1990. He also won the Macau Grand Prix, albeit controversially by hindering his rival Mika Häkkinen.

After winning Formula 3, he took an unusual step on the road to F1. It participated in the World Sports Car Championship through the Mercedes junior program, finishing fifth in the final classification despite having participated in only 30% of it. He excelled as a young driver in a championship with a high rate of veterans.

In 1991 he continued in the World Sports Car Championship finishing ninth, was fifth at Le Mans and competed in a Japanese Formula 3000 race. Finally, that same year, he would also participate in Formula 1 in the Jordan team, replacing Bertrand Gachot (who was in prison). Although he still belonged to the Mercedes program, the German team paid Jordan to let Michael compete, and thus he managed to reach the top motorsport competition.

Motorpasion.com

Conclution: Michael's road to F1 was somewhat atypical, after a 10-year stage in karting and Formula 3, his passage through other disciplines without achieving memorable successes somewhat clouded his progress, although it would not prevent him from reaching Formula 1 A score of 7/10, which could have been higher had he followed the usual path.

FERNANDO ALONSO

Alonso began his automobile career in karts, achieving his first victory at age 7 and winning the youth championships in Asturias and Galicia in 1989. Despite lacking the necessary resources to prosper, his talent helped him find financial support. to continue his career. In 1990 he won the cadet category championships of Asturias and the Basque Country and that of Spain in 1991.

He had to wait until he was old enough to compete in more powerful categories, but when he was finally able to access them he won the

Spanish Junior National Championship three consecutive times from 1993 to 1995.

His progress in karting continued with a third place in the Cadet Rainbow Trophy of the International Karting Commission, a new junior Spanish championship, the CIF-KIA 5 Continents Junior Cup in 1996 and the International Spanish A Championship in 1997. together with a second place in the European Championship and a new Spanish championship.

His success in karting would lead him to compete in the Euro Open Formula Nissan with the Campos Motorsport team in 1999 at the age of 17, getting proclaimed champion. The following year he would participate in Formula 3000 with the Astromega team, where he would get fourth place in the final classification.

By then, Cesare Fiorio, Minardi's sporting director, gave him a chance as a test driver in Formula 1. This led him to become a reserve driver in 2000, which would serve to demonstrate his talent and earn a spot as a starting driver. in 2001, thus beginning his adventure in Formula 1.

F1aescala.com

Conclution:Alonso's stage in karting was brilliant, always ahead of what his age allowed him, and that success was translated into Formula Nissan. In Formula 3000 he would not get to be champion, but he would attract the attention of Minardi, a team with which he tested and got a seat in Formula 1. He came through one of the weakest teams on the grid, which leaves his score in a 7/10.

SEBASTIAN VETTEL

After his first experiences in karting, Vettel was signed by the Red Bull Junior Team in 1998 at the age of 11, where he stood out winning various championships until in 2003 he received an offer from Derrick Walker to do private tests with single-seaters.

This led him to participate in the 2004 Formula BMW ADAC where he won the title in his first season with 18 victories out of the 20 races of the season.

The following year he signed for the ASL Mücke Motorsport team for the Formula 3 Euro Series, finishing fifth in the final standings, although winning the Rookie Cup. This allowed him to test with the Williams Formula 1 team. This in turn led him to become a test driver for BMW Sauber.

In 2006 he participated in the Formula 3 Euro Series, where he was runner-up, while he was still a Sauber tester and participated in the Formula 3.5 Series where he almost lost a finger. As a Sauber test driver, he participated in free practice for the Hungarian Grand Prix, becoming the youngest driver to participate in a Formula 1 race.

In 2007 he was leading the Formula 3.5 Series when the BMW Sauber Formula 1 team decided to have him permanently as a test driver. Following Robert Kubica's accident in Canada, Vettel had the opportunity to make his Formula 1 race debut with BMW at the United States Grand Prix finishing eighth, being the youngest driver to score points in the top car category.

Diariomotor.com

Conclution: Vettel shone in karting and in his jump to single-seater in Formula BMW ADAC. In Formula 3 Euro Series he was runner-up and came to lead the Formula 3.5 Series, also taking advantage of all the opportunities as a BMW tester, which gives him a very good progress towards Formula 1 of 8/10.

LEWIS HAMILTON

Hamilton's road to karting was an accumulation of successes. In 1995 at the age of ten he became the youngest driver to win the British karting championship. That year, Lewis Hamilton approached McLaren boss Ron Dennis to ask for an autograph and confess his desire to drive for his team in the future. Dennis told him to contact him again nine years later.

In 1999, Dennis contacted Hamilton to include him in the McLaren Young Drivers Program. A year later, Lewis won the European kart championship.

In 2001 he made the leap to single-seaters in British Formula Renault 2.0, participating in the winter series and finishing fifth in the final classification. This would be worth to him to participate in the 2002 with a complete program in the competition in the Manor equipment, being third this time. On his third attempt he would win the competition with Manor. With the championship already won and two races to go, he made his debut in the British Formula 3 Championship, participating in the last two races with little luck: a puncture in the first and an accident in the second.

In 2004 Williams was about to sign Hamilton, but the operation would not materialize since his engine supplier (BMW) did not want to finance the signing. That would see him continue his commitment to McLaren and continue to progress with Manor in Formula 3 Euro Series, where he would finish fifth. Hamilton's father pushed for Lewis to move up to the GP2 class, while McLaren preferred that he continue to gain experience in Formula 3.

The result was that in 2005 Hamilton competed in the Euro Series ASM where he would become champion (in addition to winning the Formula 3 Masters), although before that he would at least get to participate in some tests with McLaren.

In 2006 he did get promoted to GP2 where he would participate with the ART Grand Prix team, the most powerful team in the category and the current champion (thanks to Nico Rosberg). Although the favorite for the championship was Nelson Piquet Jr., Lewis Hamilton managed to take the title in his first season in the category. His victory in GP2, together with the departure of Juan Pablo Montoya and Kimi Räikkönen as McLaren's starting drivers, allowed Lewis to have a seat in Formula 1. Thus, in 2007 he would become the second McLaren driver, along with Fernando. Alonso, starting his career in Formula 1.

Okdiario.com

<u>Conclution:</u> Hamilton achieved spectacular results in karting, although it took him three years to win Formula Renault 2.0 and two to win in Formula 3. In GP2 he would win the title on the first attempt, although his ascent to Formula 1 coincided with McLaren being he was left without starting pilots facilitating having a seat, which leaves him in a progress of 7/10.

PROVISIONAL CLASSIFICATION

Name	Points
Fangio	18
Clark	16
Mansell	15
Fittipaldi	15
Prost	15
Stewart	14
Moss	12
Lauda	11
Vettel	11
Hamilton	10
Senna	10
Alonso	9
Schumacher	9

TIME TO BE CHAMPION

How long did it take each driver to become a champion once he had reached Formula 1? Obviously, the more talent, the more options to get the world title in less time, so that is a factor to take into account.

It is true that in Formula 1 not everything is merit. There are very talented drivers who take a long time to get a competent car to win a championship, either due to lack of opportunities, sponsors or because of contracts that occupy the best cars preventing their access.

Sometimes a driver capable of winning a championship has to wait too many years for a vehicle to match his talent. Luck has a lot to do with getting that well-deserved opportunity.

But it is also true that, the more talent, the more options to receive offers from winning teams and therefore the more probability of getting a seat on that machine capable of taking them to the world championship.

For this reason, the precocity when it comes to winning the world title is a factor that we cannot leave out of this analysis, and therefore we are going to study the trajectory of the drivers until they achieve that coveted world championship.

JUAN MANUEL FANGIO

As we saw before, Fangio made his debut in 1950 in the first official season of the Formula 1 World Championship with Alfa Romeo... and was about to be proclaimed champion.

He was runner-up just 3 points behind his teammate Giuseppe Farina. It should be noted that Fangio had to withdraw from three of the six championship races (if we do not count the scoring event of the Indianapolis 500 in which he did not participate), so he "won all the races in which he did not have to backing out". He equaled the champion with 3 victories, in what was a great first participation in the championship.

The following season he continued with Alfa Romeo and again won 3 rounds of the 7 races on European soil, beating not only his teammate Farina, but also the rest of the drivers, proclaiming himself champion in his second participation in the world championship. He did so by beating the legendary Alberto Ascari by 6 points.

Fromelpaddock.wordpress.com

Conclution: Fangio almost won the World Cup in his first opportunity, but he did win it in the second, so this speed in winning the title gives him a score of 9/10.

STIRLING MOSS

To speak of championships with Stirling Moss is to enter the terrain of injustice. The legendary driver is known for being the "king without a crown", and it is because, despite his great results, he did not manage to win the world championship.

His successes in Formula 1 began in 1955. Until this year he had been participating in more and more races per season. In 1955 he was runner-up with Mercedes after Fangio, and in fact it is said that Moss's glory was always overshadowed by the Argentine's talent.

In 1956 he raced with Maserati and history would repeat itself: runner-up behind Juan Manuel Fangio. Although in 1957 he would change teams to race with Vandervell, the results were repeated and he was second behind the unbeatable Fangio.

In 1958 and without Fangio in the competition, Moss finally had a chance to win, but ... he was runner-up once again, this time behind Mike Hawthorn and his Ferrari just one point apart, for more despair of the british.

From that year on, he held three third places with Walker Racing Team between 1959 and 1961 before finally retiring.

That is why, although he did not win any championship, his four runners-up and his three third places on those dates in which he was able to enjoy full seasons make him a pilot who, although he was never "the best", was always among the best three.

Elotroladodelascarreras.blog

Conclution:As he did not get the title, in this section it is not possible to rate him and in fact it is one of the reasons why many exclude him from the list of the best drivers in history. However, due to results and his ability to drive, it was mandatory to include him in this publication.

JIM CLARK

Jim Clark spent his entire career in Formula 1 with Lotus, from making his debut in 1960 to his final accident in Germany in 1968. In his first season, and despite the fact that he did not participate in four of the 10 scoring events, he took tenth place. in the classification.

From there, each year was better than the last. In 1961 he would be ranked seventh. In 1962, in addition to getting his first victories, he was runner-up 12 points behind Graham Hill. And on his fourth attempt, with 7 wins out of 9 possible and a resounding lead over Hill, he got his personal revenge and claim his first world title.

Catawiki.es

Conclution: Clark had a fast, ever-ascending trajectory, achieving a runner-up in his third season (second full) and the title in the fourth, a brilliant performance that leaves him with a score of 8/10.

JACKIE STEWART

Stewart's debut with the Owen Racing Organization in 1965 was brilliant, scoring a creditable third place in the final standings. However, the following two seasons would not be so, with a 7th and 9th place respectively, mainly due to the large number of dropouts he had to suffer, although the races he managed to finish he did with very good results, almost always in the podium or very close to it, and even with a victory.

By 1968 he changed teams looking for better luck and in Matra he found a reliability commensurate with his talent. In his first season with Matra he secured the runner-up with three victories, although somewhat far from an excellent Graham Hill. The following year the title would not escape him and he would achieve the world championship with a great advantage over the Belgian Jacky Ickx.

Chantillyartselegance.com

Conclution: Stewart made a great debut for Owen Racing, but the car's poor reliability caused him to lose three years. In Matra he got the championship on the second attempt, fifth since he arrived in Formula 1, which gives him a score of 7/10.

EMERSON FITTIPALDI

Fittipaldi also debuted with Lotus. Through the Gold Leaf Team lotus in 1970 he achieved a creditable tenth place (with victory in the United States) having participated in only 5 of the 12 races.

1971 would be his first full year in Formula 1, allowing him to improve to a final sixth place. However, it would be in 1971 at his third attempt with the John Player Team Lotus when he would surprise by getting the world title, also with a great advantage over Jackie Stewart. He became champion thanks to his five victories (that of Italy with the World Wide Racing team) and three podiums. Except for Canada, every race he finished made him in the top three.

Slotforum.com

Conclution: Fittipaldi achieved the championship in his third attempt, second with a full season, although in the previous year he was quite a long way from achieving it. A fast track to the championship that gives him a score of 8/10.

NIKI LAUDA

Lauda began to compete in 1978 with the STP March Racint Team in which he only participated in Austria where he could not finish the race. The following year he would do the full season, with a tenth place as the best race and finishing 23rd in the final classification.

He looked for better luck buying his seat at Marlboro-BRM where he would improve his results, although far from the first places: 17th in his final position.

Everything would change when he signed for Ferrari, in his first year with the Italian team he would achieve his first victories (Holland and Austria) and his first podiums. This would serve to elevate him to the fourth final position.

However, it was in 1975 when he achieved glory with Ferrari, adding 5 victories that would be enough to get the world championship over Fittipaldi, with almost 20 points of advantage.

Abc.es

Conclution: Lauda took a little longer to reach the title than other drivers, but he did so through a progressive evolution taking advantage of every opportunity and winning the championship in his fourth season if we do not count his only participation in Austria: 7/10.

NIGEL MANSELL

Mansell had a complicated Formula 1 debut, unable to finish the three races in which he was able to participate with Team Essex Lotus in 1980. In 1981 he was able to get a podium, although he would end up retiring in up to 9 races, finishing 14th.

In the same position he would finish the following season with the John Player Team Lotus, a team with which he would continue for two more years, achieving 13th and 10th.

Although he had already achieved 5 podiums with Lotus, it was when he signed for the Williams team that he began to reap his best triumphs. In 1985 and in his sixth season in Formula 1, he achieved such an evolution with the Canon Williams Honda team that he achieved victory in 2 of the last 3 races, rising to sixth place in the final classification.

His second and third years with Williams were even better, finishing runner-up in both. In 1986 it was Prost who snatched the championship from him by just two points and in 1987 Nelson Piquet beat him with a little more advantage.

His fourth season with Williams was not as productive, having to abandon in the first 7 races (which would add to the 12 total retirements) and with which he was 12th in the final classification. But at least it would help him to sign for Ferrari.

His time at Ferrari did not lead him to win the world championship either, finishing 4th in 1989 and 5th in 1990. After these results, he returned to Williams where he would enjoy a better stage with the British team.

In 1991 and back with Canon Williams, Renault was once again runner-up. This time it was Senna who gave him no chance of winning the title.

But 1992 was Mansell's most glorious year. He won the first 5 races, which would join the 9 total victories and that would finally give him that coveted drivers' title.

Autosport.com

<u>Conclution:</u>Mansell's total triumph was late. After 5 years of moderate results with Lotus and 4 years with Williams where he touched the championship on two occasions, he tried his luck at Ferrari for two seasons to return to Williams where he would finally get the championship. A long road to triumph that gives him a score of 3/10 in this section.

ALAIN PROST

Prost made his debut in an erratic stage with McLaren that took him to the 16th final position and after which he signed for Renault with whom he achieved his first victories in 1981. He spent three years in the French team, finishing 5th in the first of them, 4th in the second and runner-up in the third. In 1983 Piquet snatched the glory from him by just two points in a very tight season.

Despite the progressive evolution at Renault and having been within 2 points of achieving the championship with them, in 1984 he returned to McLaren, where with 7 victories he would repeat runner-up, this time losing the title to his teammate Niki Lauda ... half point!

Prost did not let there be a third title lost by such a small margin and in 1985 he was finally proclaimed champion with McLaren, something that he would achieve with a great advantage over Michele Alboreto.

Imgur.com

Conclution:Prost took 6 years to get the championship, although it could have been much less with several runners-up where the title eluded him by very few points. Finally, about 6 years that leave their score at 6/10.

AYRTON SENNA

Senna debuted in 1984 in a team with very few aspirations to the title such as Toleman, with which he achieved two more than worthy podiums and a 9th place in the final classification.

One season was enough to convince Lotus, with whom he achieved his first victories and was 4th in his first two seasons in the team and 3rd in the third.

With the jump to McLaren would come his first opportunities to fight for the title and he would not waste the first of them. In his first year with McLaren, 1988, with 8 victories he was proclaimed champion in a tight fight with his teammate Alain Prost.

Espn.co.uk

Conclution:Despite Senna's good results, which always exceeded expectations, it took 5 years for the Brazilian to get the world title in an always progressive trajectory. That leaves your score on this factor at 7/10.

MICHAEL SCHUMACHER

Michael made his debut in the eleventh round of the 1991 world championship with Jordan, and immediately ended the season with

Camel Benetton Ford, achieving good results that would lead him to begin a long relationship with the team.

In the following two years the victories and good results would come with Benetton, finishing 3rd in 1992 and 4th in 1993.

In 1994 an unexpected surprise came. Although Bentton had already been warning previously with the great results of the German, it was not expected that the British team would manage to lead Schumacher to the world title. However, with 8 victories and despite two disqualifications, Michael got his first championship in a fast-paced fight with Damon Hill. Both arrived with options to be proclaimed champions at the last round of the championship, but a controversial action by Schumacher seeking the collision with Hill and causing the abandonment of both, Michael was proclaimed world champion.

Diariomotor.com

Conclution:It took Schumacher only three (full) years to win his first world title. He also did it with an unexpected team. For this reason, and despite his controversial first win, a score of 8/10 is established.

FERNANDO ALONSO

Alonso made his Formula 1 debut in 2001 with Minardi, a team with which despite having no options or access to points, he performed above expectations, which led him to join Renault as a test driver.

In 2002 he convinced the French team as a tester to get a seat with which in 2003 he achieved his first victory in Hungary to finish 6th in the final classification. In 2004 he would continue his progress with Mild Seven Renault F1 Team and despite not achieving any victory, 3 podiums and a great regularity would make him climb to fourth place in the final classification.

In 2005 the year of glory would come for Alonso at Renault. With 7 victories, he would be proclaimed world champion with a certain advantage over Kimi Räikkonen's McLaren and Michael Schumacher's Ferrari.

Elconfidencial.com

Conclution: Alonso started with Minardi and as a Renault tester, two years that did not give him options for the title, but in his fourth season in Formula 1 (fifth year since his debut) he managed to be champion with an unexpected team, which gives him a score from 7/10.

SEBASTIAN VETTEL

After two years as a test driver at BMW, Vettel made his debut in 2007, replacing Kubica in the United States, which would serve to end the second half of the season with Toro Rosso, achieving a creditable fourth place in China.

2008 would be his first full season where in addition to obtaining very good results with Toro Rosso, he would get his first victory in Italy and an eighth place in the final classification. This high performance prompted Red Bull to promote him to its core team.

Already with Red Bull, he was runner-up in 2009 with four victories, just 11 points behind Jenson Button with his controversial Brawn GP. In 2010 he would expand his victories to five, which would be enough to proclaim himself world champion and begin his dominance in F1.

Diariomotor.com

Conclution: Vettel only needed three full years to be champion, added to his half season, being runner-up in one of them, in an ascending and fleeting trajectory that gives him a score of 8/10.

LEWIS HAMILTON

Lewis Hamilton made his debut in 2007 with McLaren Mercedes, a team that had been monitoring and watching over his progress as a driver. And he did so by becoming runner-up, tied on points with Alonso and... just one point behind champion Kimi Räikkonen! He got four wins in a year that was very close.

In 2008 he did manage to win the world title, which would again be decided by a single point over Felipe Massa.

Pinterest.es

Conclution: Hamilton debuted in runner-up (and by a single point difference) and clinched the title in his second year in Formula 1. Nearing perfection, his score is 9/10.

PROVISIONAL CLASSIFICATION

Driver	Points
Fangio	27
Clark	24
Fittipaldi	23
Stewart	21
Prost	21
Vettel	19
Hamilton	19
Lauda	18
Mansell	18
Senna	17
Schumacher	17
Alonso	16
Moss	12

NUMBER OF CHAMPIONSHIPS

When it comes to answering the question of who was the best driver of all time, the simplest thing would be to answer: "the one with the most world championships".

In that sense, Hamilton and Schumacher would be the best drivers in the world. But we all know that it cannot be simplified this way. A very close and contested championship is more valuable than three or four with little competition for having the best vehicle during a given stage of Formula 1.

However, while having more championships is not definitive to determine if one driver is better than another, it is a factor that we have to take into account. Winning a title is not easy, even having a very advantageous car.

Winning a championship requires perseverance, knowing how to manage the advantages and the points, it is a long-term fight through all the races that make up the season. You have to know how to think beyond, have the temperance to know when to risk and when not. You can only win multiple championships if you have those qualities. A great driver can lose a championship by risking too much and ultimately need the points he lost by being too impulsive. The most spectacular pilot does not win championships, but the most calculating one. Tell Keke Rosberg, the champion with the fewest wins in a season.

And above all, a champion must know not to lose motivation after winning the title to continue fighting for several more without losing the passion that led him to his first championship. Therefore, this is an aspect that is mandatory to analyze and score if we are looking for the best driver of all time.

JUAN MANUEL FANGIO

After his championship with Alfa Romeo in 1951, Fangio missed the 1952 season due to an accident at Monza that left him without racing for four months and after which many predicted the end of his racing career.

However, Fangio returned to racing in 1953 with Maserati and would do it in a big way, with a runner-up after failing to beat a great Alberto Ascari.

In 1954 he started with Maserati, although in the fourth race he signed for Mercedes (Daimier Benz AG) with whom he won his second world title. He would repeat the same success in 1955 to achieve his third championship.

For 1956 he signed for Ferrari. He changed team, but repeated success: fourth world title. In 1957 he returned to Maserati where once again, despite having changed vehicles, he would achieve his fifth and last world title.

Autofacil.es

Conclution: Juan Manuel Fangio achieved five world championships, giving him a score of 9/10.

STIRLING MOSS

As mentioned in the previous section, the "uncrowned king" did not win any world title, so it is not possible to score on this factor either.

JIM CLARK

After his first title in 1963 with Lotus, the following year he would be in third position. However, in 1965 he was proclaimed champion again with a small advantage over Graham Hill and giving his second title to the one known as "the flying Scotsman". This would be his last championship in a 10-year career in Formula 1 ended by an accident. in Hockenheim in which his vehicle went off the track to end up colliding with the surrounding trees.

Bbc.com

Conclution: Clark took two world titles, giving him a score of 5/10.

JACKIE STEWART

Jackie won her first championship with Matra in 1969 before joining the Tyrrell team. He would not achieve a great result in his first year with Tyrrell, ranking fifth, but in 1971 he did achieve his second world title. In 1972 he did not get the third championship, since he would be runner-up against Emerson Fittipaldi, but in 1973 he would obtain his third title.

It would be the last, since that same year, after the death of his partner Cevert, a fact that affected him notably, he decided to withdraw from the competition.

Eluniversal.com.mx

Conclution: With three world titles (and a runner-up), Stewart's score in this section is 7/10.

EMERSON FITTIPALDI

Fittipaldi could not revalidate his 1972 title with Lotus after being runner-up in 1973. This season it would be Jackie Stewart who would steal the world title from him.

In 1974 he signed for Marlboro Team Texaco (McLaren), with whom he won his second world title. The following year, as happened after his first championship, he would be runner-up again, this time in the shadow of Niki Lauda.

From there, competing with the team he founded, he would no longer be able to stay at the top of the rankings again.

Blog.20minutos.es

Conclution: with two world titles, like Clark, his score is 5/10 in this section.

NIKI LAUDA

After his 1975 championship with Ferrari, the 1976 one would escape him by just one point, a title that would go to James Hunt. Let's not forget that it was this year of his well-known and serious accident at the Nurburgring in which the flames devoured his car and part of his skin, causing his characteristic scars on his face. The smoke inhalation damaged his lungs and he was even given extreme rites. However, 40 days later he was driving his Ferrari again.

In 1977 without incidents of such caliber he would once again get his second world title with the Italian team.

After his second title, he signed with Parmalat Racing Team (Brabham) for two years before moving to McLaren in a series of mixed results, but far from his best times, it was difficult to think that Lauda would be capable of winning a new championship.

However, in 1984 and after retiring, he returned to competition to get his McLaren to the top of the rankings and win his third and last world title, a very important fact since with the so-called ground effect the cars were driven a very different way than he was used to.

Wreport.com.mx

Conclution: with three world titles (which would surely have been four without his serious accident), 7/10 points for Niki in this section.

NIGEL MANSELL

We saw earlier how hard it took Mansell to win his first world title with Williams, and he actually announced his retirement after winning it. Mansell did not want to repeat with Prost as a teammate, and in addition Williams had threatened to accept a meager contract offer since Senna himself had offered to drive for Williams for free.

Although the negotiations calmed down and Mansell would again drive in four races in 1994 for Williams and two in 1995 for McLaren, he would no longer do so with the intention of winning a second world title again.

Twsteel.com

Conclution: With a single world title, Mansell's score in this section is 3/5.

ALAIN PROST

Alain Prost would be able to revalidate in 1986 the title obtained in 1985 with Mclaren. 1987 would not be a good year for the Frenchman, fourth in the standings, but in 1988 he would be close to the top positions again, finishing runner-up after his teammate Senna.

In 1989 he would take revenge on the Brazilian in their private duel to win his third world title, before signing for Ferrari.

In his first season with the Italian team, he would lose again in his personal fight against Senna, finishing runner-up behind the Brazilian. His second year with Ferrari would finish him fifth in the standings.

After his frustrating time at Ferrari, he competed one last season in Formula 1 with the Williams team, with which he managed to achieve his fourth and final world championship in 1993.

Blogs.20minutos.es

Conclution: With 4 championships achieved, well deserved in his intense fight with Senna, his score in this section is 8/10.

AYRTON SENNA

Ayrton Senna began in 1988 with his first title, a glorious stage for him, only interrupted in 1989 by Alain Prost. Although that season he was beaten by his French partner, in 1990 and 1991 he did manage to add two more consecutive championships to reach his three personal titles.

In 1992 he would be fourth and in 1993 again runner-up after falling behind his eternal rival Alain Prost, this one already in Williams.

In 1994 he got a seat in Williams, the most desired car of the moment, with which a new horizon was opened for the infinite talent of the Brazilian. However, the tragic Tamburello curve at the Imola circuit, San Marino, prevented what would undoubtedly have been a new stage of glory for what, according to many, was the man who had the most ability to drive a Formula 1.

Primicias.ec

Conclution:three were the championships for Senna who had to compete against an impressive Alain Prost. Although without a doubt they would have been more if not for his premature end, his three titles give him a score of 7/10 in this section.

MICHAEL SCHUMACHER

If we talk about the number of championships, the kaiser has a lot to say. In 1995 Michael returned to revalidate the world title that he had achieved the previous year with Benetton. After two championships in a row, he signed for Ferrari.

In his first year in the Italian team he could only be third, although in the second year in Ferrari he would achieve the runner-up ... until he was disqualified for his reckless act when trying to cause the collision of Jacques Villeneuve to try to snatch the title from him in the last race. In his third year at Ferrari he achieved a new runner-up, this time legal, being surpassed by Mika Häkkinen, and in his fourth season he was fifth in what already seemed like a bad decision to have left Benetton.

But from the year 2000 came the well-known history of Michael Schumacher with Ferrari: five consecutive titles of absolute dominance of the kaiser with the Italian team to take him to his seven total personal titles.

Elintra.com.ar

Conclution: seven championships, a record to date, give the kaiser a score of 10/10.

FERNANDO ALONSO

After the unexpected championship of Fernando Alonso in 2005 with Renault, the Spaniard returned to repeat the title in 2006. This double championship would lead him to sign for McLaren where he would finish third, before returning two years to Renault with 5th and 9th places in the final classification.

In 2010 he signed for Ferrari for 6 years, in what was a new opportunity to fight for the title. However, he had to settle for three runners-up. In 2010 and 2012 he lost the title by four points and three points respectively against Vettel in the best Red Bull era. In 2013 it would also be Vettel who would snatch the title from him, this time with more advantage.

After his time at Ferrari, Alonso returned to McLaren at a time when the British team could not be competitive, which meant that Alonso could not add more titles to the two he owned.

Elimparcial.es

Conclution: With two world championships (and three runners-up against the best Red Bull ever), Alonso's score is 6/10.

SEBASTIAN VETTEL

After the first title with Red Bull in 2010, they would arrive three more in a row for a total of four championships driving the incredible Red Bull of Adrian Newey. In 2014 he would no longer be able to be so competitive with the energy drink team, finishing in 5th place, after which he would sign for Ferrari.

Although he won two runners-up (2017 and 2018) with the Italian team in the shadow of Hamilton, he did not win any more titles in his time with Ferrari.

Headtopics.com

Conclution: With four titles and two runners-up, Vettel deserves a very good score of 8/10 in this section.

LEWIS HAMILTON

Lewis Hamilton claimed his first title in his second season in Formula 1 with McLaren, although the following four seasons with the British team were not as productive, alternating fourth and fifth places.

That led him to sign for Mercedes, with a first year in fourth position, and from which he would begin his stage of absolute dominance of the hybrid era, achieving six more championships with the German team, only interrupted by the victory of his teammate Rosberg in the 2016 by only 5 points of difference.

Elnacional.com

Conclution: The title with McLaren, along with the 6 with Mercedes, add up to a total of seven that equals Schumacher's maximum record and gives him a total score of 10/10.

PROVISIONAL CLASSIFICATION

Driver	Points
Fangio	36
Clark	29
Prost	29
Hamilton	29
Stewart	28
Fittipaldi	28
Vettel	27
Schumacher	27
Lauda	25
Senna	24
Alonso	22
Mansell	21
Moss	12

CHAMPIONSHIPS WITH DIFFERENT BUILDERS

Winning many championships is not indicative of being the best many times. It may happen that successive titles can be chained simply by having the best vehicle during a long period.

This is one of the most criticized aspects of Lewis Hamilton, who is doubted that he could not have won so many championships without the absolute dominance of Mercedes in the hybrid era. Also Red Bull had a dominating car that favored Vettel, and even Ferrari enjoyed its victorious stage alongside Schumacher.

How much of a win is for the driver and how much for the vehicle? Obviously, Formula 1 is state-of-the-art technology, it seeks the maximum development of the car by each manufacturer and is a showcase in this regard. Behind the pilot are hundreds of engineers who do the real work of this category, the result of which is what we see on the track.

It is not conceivable to seek equality between cars as in other categories, because it would break the essence of Formula 1: the competition to develop the fastest car.

Therefore, the vehicle has a huge weight in success, many studies put it above 85%. For this reason also, a driver capable of showing that he can be a champion with several different cars, is showing that his talent is above that of the machine.

And that is what we are going to analyze in the next factor.

JUAN MANUEL FANGIO

Fangio won his first world championship with Alfa Romeo and his second in a combination of 3 races with Maserati and the rest with Mercedes (Daimier Benz AG). With the Germans he would also achieve his third title and the fourth he achieved in his only year with Ferrari, to return to Maserati and get his last and fifth championship.

In total, he was champion with up to four different cars, something that no one else has achieved in history. Coupled with a time when the pilot still had more weight in the absence of electronic or other aids, it gives him a score in this regard of 10/10.

Parabrisas.perfil.com

JIM CLARK

Clark spent his entire career with Lotus, earning him two titles with the British team. We cannot know what he would have achieved with another vehicle, so his score is 3/10.

JACKIE STEWART

Stewart got his first title with Matra, but the next two would be with Tyrrell. With BRM, in addition, he had already achieved a third place. That gives it a pretty interesting and diverse track record in terms of vehicles, with a score of 6/10.

Snaplap.net

EMERSON FITTIPALDI

Fittipaldi won his first world championship in 1972 with Lotus. The following year he would be runner-up, widely surpassed by Stewart, after which he decided to sign for McLaren.

In his first year with McLaren he was proclaimed champion again, and again the following season he would be runner-up, this time surpassed by Niki Lauda.

Later he would race in his own team where he could no longer achieve the good previous results. In total, two championships with two different constructors, giving it a score of 5/10.

Topgear.es

NIKI LAUDA

Niki Lauda won two championships during his time at Ferrari, which could easily have been three without his famous Nurburgring crash. He then raced for the Brabham team with no major successes before signing for McLaren. Of his 4 years in the British team, only one of them would be saved, 1985, in which he resurfaced to get his third and last championship. His wins with two different constructors give him a score of 5/10.

Quadis.es

NIGEL MANSELL

Nigel Mansell got a single world championship with Williams. Neither with Ferrari nor with Lotus did he repeat such success despite having certain opportunities. That gives it a score of 2/10.

Autoevolution.com

ALAIN PROST

Despite the runner-up with Renault, Alain Prost had a great stage at McLaren where he won his first three championships. His subsequent passage through Ferrari was not so glorious, although he got the runner-up in 1990 very close to his former teammate Senna.

In his last season at Williams he won his last World Cup to be proclaimed champion with two different teams, which could have been three had he not suffered from the competition of a huge Senna. This gives it a score of 7/10.

Diariomotor.com

AYRTON SENNA

Senna achieved his three titles with McLaren. Previously with Lotus he had achieved a third place. Had he not suffered his fatal accident, he would most likely have won another title with another manufacturer, and his signing for Williams was a great opportunity for that. But that is something that we can never know and that leaves you in this section with a score of 2/10.

MICHAEL SCHUMACHER

His first two titles with Benetton were a prelude to what Michael could achieve with a more powerful team. That way, he would later achieve the five championships in a row with Ferrari.

On his return to Formula 1 with a Mercedes that was still a long way from the one that would dominate the hybrid era, he failed to perform at his best, with an 8th as the best final position and always behind his teammate Rosberg.

Therefore, seven titles with two teams give it a score of 6/10.

Elboletin.com

FERNANDO ALONSO

Fernando Alonso achieved his two championships with Renault. He also came close to achieving it three times with Ferrari and was 3rd with McLaren. That gives it a score of 4/10.

Matraxlubricantes.com

SEBASTIAN VETTEL

The German won four championships, but they were all driving a Red Bull. During his time at Ferrari, he got two runners-up, always in the shadow of Hamilton. Being a winner with a constructor, although almost getting it with a second on two occasions, his score is also 4/10.

Tresruedas.wordpress.com

LEWIS HAMILTON

Hamilton debuted as champion with Mclaren. When Mclaren showed signs that he was beginning to be far from his past glory, he made the wise decision to sign for a Mercedes team that was still far from dominating the hybrid era, and where he won six more titles.

Absolute dominance with one constructor and a championship (and runner-up) with another give him a score of 6/10.

Hondusports.com

PROVISIONAL CLASSIFICATION

Fangio	46
Prost	36
Hamilton	35
Stewart	34
Fittipaldi	33
Schumacher	33
Clark	32
Vettel	31
Lauda	30
Senna	26
Alonso	26
Mansell	23
Moss	12

MATCHES AGAINST TEAMMATES

Formula 1 is technology and the performance of the car has a lot to do with success. One vehicle is more likely to make a champion driver than the other way around. That is why it is so difficult to know who is the best driver in history.

But the pilots who compete in the same team, do so with the same car. In equal conditions. That is why the main rival of a pilot is his own teammate. If you are constantly beaten with the same vehicle ... It is the benchmark against which one driver can measure himself over another.

It is true that in many cases the cars of the same team are not the same. The pieces or the evolutions do not arrive in the same order and can always favor one of your pilots. But it is in the talent and the authority of each driver to win favoritism within the team itself.

And that is what we are going to analyze in this section. We are going to compare the drivers with their colleagues throughout their careers so that, regardless of the team they were in, we will know when they were superior by simple talent and their own characteristics with a rival on equal terms.

JUAN MANUEL FANGIO

In his debut in Formula 1 in 1950 Fangio was surpassed by his partner Farina in Alfa Romeo, although he was ahead of Luigi Fagioli (the rest of the team's drivers only participated in isolation).

In 1951 he was champion and took revenge on his partner Farina, also being ahead of his other teammates who participated in practically the entire season in Toulo de Graffenried and Consalvo Sanesi.

In 1953 with Maserati he was runner-up, but managed to be above his two companions, the Argentine José Froilán González and Felice Bonetto.

In his two seasons at Mercedes he was proclaimed champion on both occasions, being ahead of teammates such as the Germans Karl Kling and Hans Hermann and also Stirling Moss.

At Ferrari he would once again be champion over Eugenio Castellotti, Luigi Musso and Peter Collins, and on his return to Maserati he beat all the teammates of the extensive Italian team, such as Jean Behra, Carlos Menditéguy or Harry Schell. After that I would no longer race in Formula 1 continuously.

In short, in his career in Formula 1, he was only beaten once by one of his teammates, which gives him a score of 9/10.

Formulaf1.es

STIRLING MOSS

Stirling Moss began racing continuously in Formula 1 in the 1955 season at Mercedes. This year he lagged behind Fangio, but beat Karl Kling on the German team.

In 1956 and already in Maserati, he would once again be in the shadow of Fangio, but he was the best driver of the Officine Alfieri Maserati team ahead of Frenchman Jean Behra and Italian Cesare Perdisa. In 1957 something similar would happen, once again behind Fangio in the championship, but being the best of his team, now Vanwall, surpassing Tony Brooks.

In 1958 he would once again be the best Vanwall driver again ahead of Tony Brooks and Stuart Lewis-Evans in a team made up of three Brits.

In 1959 he raced with the Walker Racing Team to be ahead of his only partner, Frenchman Maurice Trintignant, despite the fact that he ran two races less than him.

In 1960 he did not run a full program and in his final season in 1961 he was the only driver to run every race for the Walker team.

This means that he was the best driver in his team throughout his career except in 1955 where he was left behind at Mercedes by the man who snatched the opportunity to win a Formula 1 title: Juan Manuel Fangio. 9/10.

Autoblog.com.ar

JIM CLARK

In Clark's first full season at Lotus, 1961, he lagged just behind teammate Innes Ireland, just one point behind, largely due to the latter's victory in the last grand prix.

In 1962 he changed his teammate at Lotus, Trevor Taylor, whom he surpassed with a wide advantage, and whom he would again surpass with an even greater difference in 1963; 54 points (year in which he was champion) against a single point from Taylor.

In 1964 he did not have a partner to measure himself against, Clark was the only permanent Lotus driver along with colleagues who participated partially such as Peter Arundell or Mike Spence. In 1965 Spence participated in equal number of races, but was 44 points behind Clark.

In 1966 Lotus tested several engines and chassis, as well as a large staff of five drivers, of which Jim Clark was once again the most prominent, something similar to what happened the following season.

Clark was only behind a teammate in one season, while the rest not only beat them, but did so with a wide advantage: 9/10.

Jimclarktrust.com

JACKIE STEWART

In his first season at Owen Racing, he only had the great Graham Hill as a teammate, falling immediately behind him in the final standings. He also failed to overtake him in 1966, where Hill was 5th and Stewart 7th. In his third year at BRM, he switched partners to Mike Spence, whom he did manage to beat, albeit by a single point.

Already on his arrival in Matra, Stewart beat the French Servoz-Gavin and Beltoise with much difference over both. In his second year he would maintain the difference with Beltoise before signing for Tyrrell.

In his first year at Tyrrell he was the only driver who participated throughout the entire championship, but in the second he would have François Cevert as a partner, whom he doubled in score. This duel would be repeated in 1972, this time tripling the Frenchman's points, and also in 1973 maintaining a great advantage.

While his time at BRM was tough against Graham Hill, his lead against his teammates at Matra and Tyrrell was very prominent, giving him a score of 8/10.

Sfcriga.com

EMERSON FITTIPALDI

The first year at Lotus, Fittipaldi "only" managed to finish sixth in the standings, but he did so well ahead of his teammate, the Swede Reine Wisell. In 1972, David Walker joined the team, but while the Australian did not score any points, Fittipaldi was proclaimed champion. In 1973 he met a tougher partner at Lotus: Ronnie Peterson. However, he also managed to surpass him, although only by 3 points.

Already at McLaren, his first great rival and partner was Denny Hulme, which he led by 25 points. In 1975 his partner at McLaren was Jochen Mass. While the Brazilian was champion, Mass was 8th in the standings.

Regarding his stage with his own team, in 1976 Fittipaldi got 3 points while his teammate Ingo Hoffmann failed to score. In 1977, Hoffmann only participated in two races. In 1978 Emerson decided to compete without companions and in 1979 the Brazilian Alex Ribeiro only accompanied him in two tests. In his final season, Fittipaldi did have Keke Rosberg, who beat him by a single point before the Brazilian's retirement.

Keke, future Formula 1 champion, was the only one capable of beating a Fittipaldi who beat drivers of the stature of Peterson and Hulme, therefore he deserves no less than a score of 9/10.

Pinterest.co.uk

NIKI LAUDA

Niki's first full season in March was disastrous, failing to score while teammate Ronnie Peterson did manage to score a dozen points.

During his time at BRM in 1973 he managed to match his teammate Clay Regazzoni on points, but would be surpassed by Frenchman Jean-Pierre Beltoise.

In his first year at Ferrari, he would once again share a team with Regazzoni, a duel in which the Swiss was the winner. The couple would repeat in 1975 where the result would be reversed, being Lauda champion. In the fateful year of 1976, and despite the Austrian's difficulties, he again beat Regazzoni. In his last year at Ferrari he would have as his main partner the Argentine Carlos Reutemann, whom he also managed to overcome.

At Brabham his first partner was John Watson, whom he easily beat, and in his second season he would have Nelson Piquet as a teammate, who he also managed to beat by one point in a not very competitive car.

After his signing for McLaren he met again with John Watson, but this time the British would be the winner of the duel. Watson would also get better results than Lauda in 1983. In 1984 his McLaren partner was Alain Prost, in one of the fiercest duels in Formula 1: Lauda was champion by just half a point ahead of the Frenchman. However, in 1985 it was Prost who most prominently defeated Lauda before his final retirement.

While Niki was superior to her peers in her time at Ferrari and Brabham, she was less so at BRM AND McLaren where she was not as consistent, hence a score of 6/10.

NIGEL MANSELL

Mansell's first teammate in his first full season at Lotus was the Italian Elio de Angelis, against whom he was widely outclassed. In 1983 Lotus repeated the lineup, but this time it was Mansell who beat his partner. 1984 was the year of the "tiebreaker", and this third time it was Elio who defeated Mansell in an outstanding way.

In 1985, Nigel's first season at Williams, he coincided with Keke Rosberg, who finished third while Mansell could only be 6th. In 1986 his partner in Williams would be Nelson Piquet, whom he was able to overcome, albeit by a single point. This duel was repeated in 1987 where both would be at the top of the championship, but the Brazilian being the champion. After Piquet's departure to Lotus, his partner in Williams would become the Italian Riccardo Patrese, whom he surpassed in a mediocre season for the British team.

After his signing for Ferrari, he shared a team with Gerhard Berger, obtaining better results than the Austrian. In his second year in red he had Alain Prost as a partner, a tougher rival who almost doubled him in points.

On his return to Williams he met Patrese again, with Mansell 2nd and the Italian 3rd in the standings. In 1992, the year in which Mansell was champion, both achieved the first and second places in the classification. After the title, Mansell did not compete again for a full season.

His duels with teammates were somewhat irregular, he came out losing at Lotus, and then he was overtaken by drivers of the stature of Rosberg, Piquet and Prost. However, he outscored Berger and Patrese, giving him a score of 4/10.

ALAIN PROST

In his first season Prost lost in his personal duel with John Watson, but he did so by a single point and taking into account that Watson ran one more race than him.

In his first year at Renault, he easily beat the Frenchman René Arnoux, whom he beat again in 1982 more closely. In 1983 his partner at Renault was Eddie Cheever, who was no match for him.

At McLaren he met a champion Niki Lauda in an exciting season in which the Austrian won by just half a point. The following year he took revenge by beating a Niki who would have a difficult season. In 1986 his partner was Keke Rosberg, whom he notably surpassed. In 1987 he beat the Swede Stefan Johansson, this one by only 4 points. In 1988 he shared a team at McLaren with Ayrton Senna, leading to one of the most legendary matches in Formula 1. The Brazilian beat him by just 3 points, to reverse positions in 1989 before signing for Ferrari.

Prost beat Mansell, his first Ferrari teammate and also Jean Alesi, second teammate in the Italian team.

In his last season, at Williams, he was proclaimed champion over his teammate Damon Hill. Prost only lost against Watson in his first year (and with one career less), and then against great champions like Niki Lauda and Ayrton Senna, whom he later surpassed. Being at the level of the best, his score is 8/10.

Autobild.es

AYRTON SENNA

In his debut at Toleman, he was the only driver who ran the entire season with the team, but at Lotus he would have his first confrontation with Elio de Angelis, who he beat by 5 points. In 1986 his partner at Lotus was Johnny Dumfries; Senna had 55 points while Dumfries only had three. Senna closed his stage at Lotus beating the Japanese Satoru Nakajima... with a 50-point advantage!

His first two years at McLaren ended in a dueling tie with Alain Prost and the following three seasons in the British team he would consecutively beat a Gerhard Berger who could only be competitive in the last of them, remaining one point behind the Brazilian. His last year at McLaren alternated teammates: Andretti and Mika Häkkinen.

In Williams he started the season with Damon Hill, but bad fortune in San Marino deprived the fans of this great personal duel.

Senna not only beat his teammates, but often did so with a huge advantage and only found in Prost an opponent to match, giving him a score of 9/10.

Carburando.com

MICHAEL SCHUMACHER

In 1992 Michael was running his first season in Formula 1 with Benetton and Martin Brundle as a teammate, which he surpassed with a certain advantage. In his second season at Benetton, his partner would be Riccardo Patrese, who he also beat comfortably. In 1994 his rival was supposed to be JJ Lehto, but a broken vertebra caused his replacement, Jos Verstappen, to participate in more races than him. In any case, the only one to do the full season was Michael. In his last year at Benetton his partner and rival was Johnny Herbert, whom he also beat widely.

In 1996 he signed for Ferrari to share a team with Eddie Irvine, scoring 59 points against 11 for the Briton. In 1997 and 1998 he again beat Irvine (although Michael's 1997 points were canceled), and in 1999 an accident in Great Britain prevented him from completing the season. Between 2000 and 2004 he won the 5 consecutive titles for Ferrari, always ahead of his teammate Rubens Barrichello. Even in 2005, where the Ferrari seemed not to be doing so well, it beat the Brazilian. In 2006 Felipe Massa was his new partner, whom he also managed to overcome before his first retirement.

On his return with Mercedes between 2010 and 2012, he failed to adapt and was beaten on all three occasions by the German Nico Rosberg. Therefore, Michael was superior to all his teammates who could only overcome him by disqualification or accident ... at least until his return in 2010, which is the only thing that tarnishes his personal duels with a 9/10 rating.

Grandprix247.com

FERNANDO ALONSO

In his debut with Minardi, Alonso shared a team with Tarso Marques, and Alex Yoong in the last three races. Neither managed to score, but Brazilian Marques achieved the best final result in a race that season: 9th.

At Renault he met Jarno Trulli, whom he surpassed in his first two seasons with the French team, and Giancarlo Fisichella, whom he also beat in the next two.

At McLaren he faced an unexpected Lewis Hamilton whom he equaled on points, but lagging behind him in number of victories.

On his return to Renault he had no difficulty overcoming a Nelson Piquet Jr. who, in season two, was replaced by Grosjean.

In his first 4 years at Ferrari he shared a team with Massa, beating him in all of them. The fifth featured Räikkonen as a teammate, whom he also vastly outscored before signing for McLaren.

His first partner on his return to McLaren was Jenson Button, who managed to get 5 points more than the Spanish. In 2016 it would be Fernando who won the duel (despite running one less race). Finally, in his last two years at McLaren, Alonso would be ahead of Belgian Stoffel Vandoorne. Outperformed by Marques, Hamilton and Button on three different teams, his score is 7/10.

Revistasafetycar.com

SEBASTIAN VETTEL

In 2008 Vettel completed his first full season at Toro Rosso over and above his partner Bourdais. Already in Red Bull, he beat Mark Webber between 2009 and 2013 without giving the Australian any option in the 5 years. In 2014 his new partner was Ricciardo, who did manage to beat the German before he left for Ferrari.

In 2015 his first Ferrari teammate was Kimi Räikkonen, whom he beat both that year and the next three. Only the arrival of the talented Leclerc to Ferrari could end Vettel's personal duel victories at Ferrari. The Monegasque was ahead of the German in 2019 and 2020.

Only beaten by Ricciardo and Charles Leclerc, Vettel has an enviable winning record against all his teammates with a score of 8/10.

Speedcafe.com

LEWIS HAMILTON

Hamilton debuted in style in Formula 1, finishing in McLaren above his teammate Fernando Alonso (although they were even on points). After the Spanish left, his partner at McLaren was Heikki Kovalainen, whom he surpassed in 2008 and 2009 before the arrival of Jenson Button. Button was a tougher rival, Hamilton won the first duel, but in 2011 Jenson would be the best McLaren driver. In 2012 Hamilton managed to tie the tie in a very tight way in the British duel before signing for Mercedes.

In the German team he met Nico Rosberg, who had just overtaken Schumacher, but whom he beat in the first three seasons. Nico managed to make amends in 2016 by beating Hamilton, before retiring due to excessive pressure. From 2017 to 2020, Hamilton's partner was Finn Valtteri Bottas, a comfortable partner who he has outclassed year after year.

Hamilton was only beaten throughout his career by Jenson Button (whom he would eventually surpass on aggregate at McLaren) and by Nico Rosberg, in one of the four years he shared with him at Mercedes, leaving him with a score of 8 / 10.

Elintra.com.ar

PROVISIONAL CLASSIFICATION

Name	Score
Fangio	55
Prost	44
Hamilton	43
Stewart	42
Fittipaldi	42
Schumacher	42
Clark	41
Vettel	39
Lauda	36
Senna	35
Alonso	33
Mansell	27
Moss	21

SKILL IN RAIN

When the asphalt is in wet conditions, Formula 1 becomes spectacular. Anything can happen. Any slight mistake immediately translates into an accident or abandonment. As many members of the Great Circus say, "the rain differentiates between the boys and the men at the wheel."

And it is that if already controlling a Formula 1 is a task of heroes, when it rains the difficulty multiplies. Almost all grip is lost, and driving a car with almost a thousand horsepower with almost zero grip is one of the most difficult and dangerous things in the world.

But the rain also equalizes the cars. Unable to develop their full potential on water, they left the victory to the pilots. Talent when driving becomes even more essential when it rains.

In wet asphalt conditions personal talent prevails when driving over the characteristics of the machine. For this reason, it is a factor that we have to take into account in the search for the best driver of all time.

Let's look back on some of the brightest performances in wet conditions that will give these drivers some additional points for qualifying.

VETTEL: Italy 2008

Sebastian Vettel got his first victory in Formula 1 aboard a Toro Rosso that hardly had the capacity to finish in scoring positions. However, the rain at Monza gave the less prominent cars on the grid a chance to achieve great results, and the German made good use of it.

Vettel took pole position in a qualifying in the rain, and kept the first position in the first part of the race sliding the car over the recommended caution.

Vettel was helped by the weather. The rain stopped and the asphalt began to dry out, so Hamilton's bet to switch to extreme rain tires on his last change to the pits was turned against the Briton. But even so, no one hesitated to praise Vettel's driving without which the Toro Rosso would not have been able to achieve victory. 5 additional points in this regard for the German.

Racefans.net

LEWIS HAMILTON: Great Britain, 2008

The two McLarens occupied the front row of the starting grid at the rainy 2008 British Grand Prix. Driving conditions were so difficult that veteran drivers like Massa and Webber did not take a lap to make mistakes.

Meanwhile, Hamilton chased his teammate Kovalainen, closing the gap, and overtaking him on the fifth lap. From there, it began a tortuous driving with the visor constantly fogged and having to clean it often to get some vision.

After the first pit stop, Hamilton found himself chased by Räikkonen's Ferrari, who only five laps later managed to lead by 22 seconds. At the second stop McLaren risked putting intermediate tires on Hamilton, reaching a pace 3 seconds higher than those with rain tires. In worse conditions than the rest, he had to stay on the track until it began to dry out, where he regained his rhythm to end up winning with an advantage of more than one minute over the second classified. Hamilton remembers this as one of his best and most difficult races earning him 6 more points in this study.

F1experiences.com

JIM CLARK: Belgium, 1963

Clark had to face the rain on one of his least liked circuits, when by then it was 14 kilometers long. After qualifying eighth, he had an outstanding start until he was at the top of the race with the Graham Hill BRM, which he surpassed and led by eight seconds five laps later.

Clark's lead increased as the rain intensified past 20 laps. While the rest of the pilots were weakened by the harsh conditions, Clark seemed to make the most of them. Colin Chapman himself even asked for the cancellation of the race, but his request was denied.

The end result was a victory almost five minutes ahead of the runner-up in brilliant driving over rain that seemed unable to beat Jim and added an additional 7 points.

Soymotor.com

MICHAEL SCHUMACHER: Spain, 1996

The kaiser achieved his first victory with Ferrari in Spain, and had to do it with a car that was struggling to get a good pace in the dry.

In the rain, driving became impossible, with teammate Irvine going off on the second lap and Hill going off as many as three times. However, by lap 9, Schumacher had already climbed from sixth to second. A little later, he would end up overtaking Jacques Villeneuve and increasing his lead as the leader lap after lap.

Schumacher, with more insistence than the rest of the riders, constantly changed the line looking for the best possible grip, risking in conditions that made him have to retire half of the grid.

Everyone applauded Schumacher's driving skills and his ability to handle a very difficult Ferrari to drive on an ice-like track. Michael would string together numerous additional wet successes throughout his career, earning 8 points for his talent in the water.

Diariomotor.com

JACKIE STEWART: Germany, 1968

Stewart ended up winning in very difficult conditions at the "most difficult circuit of all time", the 22-kilometer Nurburgring.

Stewart started in third row, reaching third position at the start with his Matra. To do this, he looked for the pavement of the pitlane to have more grip than on the asphalt of the track.

Before the first lap ended, he managed to pass Chris Amon and Graham Hill and gain an eight-second lead. On lap eight, Stewart was 15 seconds behind the fastest second on that lap. Adding to this magnificent driving on one of the most terrible circuits to run in the rain is the difficulty of doing it with a broken wrist. Not a few are the fans who remember this performance as the most brilliant on rain, which gives the Briton 9 additional points.

Dandydriver.com

AYRTON SENNA: Portugal, 1985

When it comes to driving in rainy conditions, one name pops into the minds of all Formula 1 fans: Ayrton Senna. And although there are several performances in the wet that could be chosen, the Estoril of 1985 is undoubtedly one of the most outstanding in the history of this discipline.

Senna took the first pole of his career in Portugal and took advantage of it properly to lead his teammate Elio de Angelis by almost 3 seconds before finishing the first lap. His lead increased even more until mid-race conditions worsened noticeably. Senna himself tried to request the cancellation with gestures, but the competition continued.

The track conditions were as complicated as they were changing, which made it difficult to estimate a minimally safe line, each lap was different from the previous one, which caused that without references only 9 drivers out of 26 managed to finish the race. The most shocking thing was that, while everyone tried to stay on track as best they could, Senna ended up bending one after another with his Lotus, only sparing Michele Alboreto's Ferrari from being bent.

The previous year, Senna had already warned with the Toleman, and may have won a race in Monaco that was controversially suspended due to harsh rain conditions. Without a doubt, a historic rider who when the track got wet "made the rest seem mediocre." 10 additional points for the Brazilian magician.

Autobild.es

PROVISIONAL CLASSIFICATION

Fangio	55
Stewart	51
Schumacher	50
Hamilton	49
Clark	48
Senna	45
Prost	44
Vettel	44
Fittipaldi	42
Lauda	36
Alonso	33
Mansell	27
Moss	21

DEVELOPMENT OF THE MONOPLAZA

One of the great characteristics that every great driver must have is his ability to provide information to the team to improve the car. Many times a driver is accused of being "lucky to get to a winning team with an advantageous car", and his victories are detracted for having achieved them through a winning car.

This argument is suffered by drivers like Hamilton or Vettel, belonging to a modern era where teams have managed to dominate Formula 1 thanks to an advantageous car for several years.

The opposite occurs with the pilots of the first years of Formula 1, where the teams barely had a couple of mechanics and did not have large facilities with hundreds of workers taking care of the development of the car.

But there is no doubt that, while the driver is only the last part of a whole great structure, his contribution is vital for the vehicle's performance to improve. He must be able to convey his needs so that they provide him with a car adapted to his qualities and suggest effective changes, as well as know how to convey his behavior on the track. It must also have the necessary consistency lap by lap to be able to make effective comparisons and analyzes that could not be done with irregular driving and offering little useful results.

In this section we are going to analyze how they got to the teams and in what position they left them, to see if their passage through them helped the teams to develop or, on the contrary, they got worse.

JUAN MANUEL FANGIO

Fangio joined Alfa Romeo in 1950, the first year of the competition, so it is difficult to have previous references, but he was a winning car the two seasons he was on board.

In 1953 he signed for a Maserati that had not participated in the first three races of the previous season and with which he got second place.

In 1954 and 1955 he drove for Mercedes, which had not previously participated in the championship, so again there are no previous references, but which he made two-time champion with two consecutive titles.

In 1956 he signed for a Ferrari that the previous year had only achieved fourth place for the Frenchman Maurice Trintignant as best position and which Fangio made champion.

Lastly, Fangio returned to a Maserati that had been runner-up with Stirling Moss before he led the team back to glory.

Despite the fact that on several occasions there are no previous references to evaluate Fangio's contribution to the team, he was able to make four of them champion. It must be taken into account that Fangio acted as the main mechanic even of his own vehicle, staying on several occasions until late at night doing repairs and getting his vehicle ready for the next day. He also liked to select his accompanying mechanics himself, so that Fangio was himself the nucleus of development of the car and was fully involved in its maintenance.

Having led so many different teams to glory and with a total involvement in the vehicle, there is no doubt then of his contribution: 10/10.

STIRLING MOSS

Moss had his first stable year on a team in 1955 with Mercedes in a brand new team. In 1956 he signed for Maserati, which was coming off a difficult campaign, with the eighth place of Argentine Roberto Mieres as the best classified driver. Stirling got second place with the Italian team.

In 1957 he signed for Vanwall after a disastrous season, where his best driver had been Harry Schell, 17th. Moss was runner-up both that year and the next.

In 1959 he signed for Cooper in the Walker Racing Team, in which Maurice Trintignant had only managed to be seventh. With Moss on the team, it posted three consecutive third spots.

Therefore, Moss greatly improved the results previously achieved by the teams for which he successively signed, all of them evolved remarkably with the Briton on their roster, giving him a score of 10/10.

Statsf1.com

JIM CLARK

Jim Clark joined Lotus in 1960, after a year in which the Team Lotus team had not exactly shined, with Innes Ireland in 14th place and Graham Hill not scoring as most consistent drivers.

In his first year at Lotus, the team made a remarkable improvement. Clark was tenth while Ireland managed to move up to fourth final position. In 1961 Ireland was sixth and Clark seventh.

From there came Jim's best years, with four consecutive years finishing among the top three in Formula 1, a sixth place in 1966 and a new third step in 1967,

It can therefore be deduced that since its arrival Lotus has progressively improved its results and maintained them, except for an irregular 1967, which gives it a score of 8/10 regarding its contribution to the team.

Bbc.com

JACKIE STEWART

Stewart started his career with a BRM in very good condition, having led Graham Hill to runner-up and Richie Ginther to fifth. Stewart took advantage of the team's good form by finishing third in his first year at Owen Racing Organization, however the next two years he could not help the team to maintain the level, finishing seventh and ninth.

After this decadent career, he went to Matra International, a team that debuted as such in the competition and with which he was runner-up in his first season and champion in the second. Previously, Matra as a constructor had participated in isolated races without much success.

Finally, Stewart signed for a Tyrrell Racing Organization team that was also making its debut in the competition and did so with a fifth place, which in the next three years would lead to two championships and a runner-up.

It is difficult to know the contribution of Stewart to his teams since he joined recently created structures, but it is true that he knew how to take these new teams to the top, with the notable difficulty that this entails. However, his declining track record at BRM leaves him with a score of 7/10.

Co.pinterest.com

EMERSON FITTIPALDI

Fittipaldi joined the Lotus team in which Jochen Rindt won the champion title after losing his life at Monza practice in 1970. He could not take advantage of having a champion car and in 1971 he was sixth. However, it would help maintain the potential of the team in the next two years as champion and runner-up respectively.

Fittipaldi left Lotus at the top to join a McLaren that the previous year had only been able to provide a sixth place for Denny Hulme and that had left Jody Scheckter without scoring. Fittipaldi's talent lifted McLaren back to glory: once again, championship and runner-up in two years.

However, in the stage in which he began to participate with his own team, the results were very mixed and not very successful. Although the first three years there was an upward evolution, the fourth of them Fittipaldi was 21st.

His ability to keep Lotus high (despite a mediocre year) and to bring McLaren back to the top, coupled with his inability to develop his own team give him a score of 6/10.

Infobae.com

NIKI LAUDA

Lauda made his first full season in 1972 at STP March Racing Team, after a year in which Swede Ronnie Peterson had been runner-up with the team. With a initially competent vehicle, Niki Lauda was 23rd and Peterson 9th, in a clear decline in team performance.

In 1973 he joined BRM, a team whose best driver the previous season had been Howden Ganley in 13th place with 4 points. Niki Lauda was 17th with only 2 points.

In 1974 he signed for a Ferrari that had just finished 9th with Jacky Ickx and 12th with the Italian Arturo Merzario. In this case, Niki was a blessing for the Italian team, who returned to win titles and did not drop from fourth place with Lauda as driver. His contributions to improving the car are also known from this stage, since his partner Regazzoni was able to improve his times with Lauda's Ferrari by up to more than two seconds compared to his own.

Lauda then joined a Brabham far from his best times, and managed to raise it to third place in constructors, although in his second season he dropped to eighth.

Finally, Lauda returned to Formula 1 with a McLaren in sixth place in the team classification and was champion again with the British team, with which he did not have a good last year in 1985 although he would help maintain the constructors' title.

Lauda worsened the performance of his early BRM and March teams, although he did help restore glory to Ferrari and McLaren. That gives it a score of 7/10.

NIGEL MANSELL

Mansell had his first full season in a Lotus that was coming off fifth in the constructors' standings. During his first three years with the team, the constructor ranged from fifth to eighth, although in Mansell's final year he managed to establish himself among the top three.

Nigel then signed for a Williams who by then had been in sixth position. In his first year with the British Williams rose to third position and was champion in the second and third, although in his final year in the first stage Williams the team collapsed to seventh position.

By then, Mansell signed for Ferrari, which had achieved the constructors' runner-up. In its first year in red the Italian team slipped to third place, although it regained the runner-up in 1990 before Mansell's return to a Williams who by then was fourth in the constructors' standings. On his return to the British team, Williams rose to runner-up, to win a new constructors' title in 1992, the year in which Mansell permanently stopped participating in Formula 1.

It can therefore be said that Mansell helped Lotus return to the top positions and took Williams to the top twice, although in his time at Ferrari his team neither improved nor worsened. That gives him a good team contribution score of 8/10.

Clarin.com

ALAIN PROST

Alain Prost began his career in Formula 1 in a McLaren team that had been the seventh constructor... and that already with Prost dropped to ninth place.

The Frenchman then signed for Renault, which was positioned far above, fourth behind Williams, Ligier and Brabham. In Alain's first two years at the French manufacturer, Renault rose to third place and was runner-up in the third. So, Prost returned to a McLaren better positioned than in his first year in the competition: fifth.

On his return to the British team, Prost would collaborate with Niki Lauda to win the championship for McLaren. The title would be repeated in 1985, although it would descend to second place in 1986 and 1987 to regain the throne in 1988, the year after which Prost signed for the runner-up: Ferrari.

With Prost in their ranks, Ferrari would once again repeat runner-up and fall into third position in the Frenchman's second season, which would make him sign for Williams, a runner-up who Prost would help win the title in 1993.

Bottom line: after a poor first year at McLaren, Prost helped progressively improve Renault, returned to McLaren to keep it in the title fight (and get it) for five years before a not very productive spell with Ferrari, after which it would help Williams become champion again. A great contribution to his various teams that his poor time at Ferrari gives him a score of 8/10.

Biografiasyvidas.com

AYRTON SENNA

Senna made his debut for the Toleman team that had been ninth the season before his signing. With Senna as the driver, the British manufacturer rose to seventh position.

His talent in a low-class team led the Brazilian to join the Lotus team when it occupied third place in the constructors' list below Ferrari and McLaren. Lotus was 4th, 3rd and 3rd respectively with Senna in their ranks, so the Brazilian only helped the constructor to maintain his trajectory.

It was then that Senna signed for the runner-up manufacturer of the moment: McLaren. With Ayrton on their roster, the British team won no less than four consecutive constructors' titles, and two runners-up in their final seasons before signing for Williams. Unfortunately, with Williams Senna he was only able to participate in three races, without being able to finish any of them.

Senna improved a Toleman team that hardly dreamed of the results the Brazilian provided, helped Lotus stay in the top three and achieved a glorious stage with six-year McLaren in which he helped create a hegemony stage with four. titles and two runners-up, giving it a score of 9/10.

Gascommunity.com

MICHAEL SCHUMACHER

Schumacher raced his first full season in Formula 1 for a Benetton team that had just been the fourth constructor in the standings (a result he had contributed to by running the last five races of 1991). In 1992 Benetton rose to third place, maintained it in 1993, achieved runner-up in 1994 and finally won the constructors' title in 1995 thanks to an evolution in which the kaiser had much to contribute.

Michael then signed for Ferrari, which by then was the third manufacturer. In its first three years in red, Ferrari took the runner-up, finally claiming the title in 1999. It would be the first of five more constructors' titles with Michael Schumacher on their roster until 2004, marking a golden run for Ferrari. In 2005, the year before its first retirement, Ferrari fell to third place.

His return to Formula 1 in 2010 with Mercedes would not be so glorious. Michael announced his celebrated return to competition in a new team that had acquired the reigning champion, Brawn GP. Mercedes was 4th the first two years with Michael, and 5th the season of the German's final retirement.

Michael led Benetton to the championship and allowed Ferrari to regain glory to establish one of the most brilliant stages of the Italian team. Only his poor comeback with Mercedes prevents a total score, 9/10 for the kaiser.

Sopitas.com

FERNANDO ALONSO

Fernando Alonso made his debut with Minardi, a team at the end of the grid that had finished 10th the previous season without scoring. In 2001 his result would not be much different, last in the classification without scoring any points again.

In 2002 Alonso became a Renault reserve driver, the year in which the French team finished fourth. Already with Alonso as the starting driver in 2003, Renault maintained fourth position, rose to third in 2004 and would take an incredible leap, winning the constructors' titles in 2005 and 2006. After his feat at Renault, Alonso signed for McLaren, which was the third team. of the moment. Together with Hamilton, he won a constructors' title that ... would later be annulled for espionage.

Alonso decided to return to Renault which had fallen to third place since his departure, although he was unable to help stop this decline, the team came fourth in 2008 and eighth in 2009.

After the crash of Renault, Alonso announced his signing for Ferrari, which in 2009 had finished fourth, far from its usual glory. Already in his first year with the Italian team, Ferrari recovered the third position, which it held in 2011. In 2012 it achieved the runner-up position unable to overcome Red Bull, but in 2013 it would also be surpassed by the Mercedes team. In 2014, Alonso's last year at Ferrari, the team returned to fourth place again.

Alonso then decided to return to McLaren, which with a fifth position was moving away from its most glorious times. Fernando's four years at McLaren were very irregular, alternating sixth and ninth places in the constructors' world championship. Thus, Alonso contributed to Renault's first and only titles and returned McLaren to the top constructors spot (as it would lose in the offices). However, his second stage at Renault would coincide with three years of decline, at Ferrari he seemed to glimpse some improvement that ended up fading and on his return to McLaren the British team reaped one of the worst times in its history. For all this, a score of 5/10.

SEBASTIAN VETTEL

Vettel raced the second half of the 2007 season with Toro Rosso, the year Red Bull's second team finished seventh in the standings. In his first full season with the team, he rose to sixth position, after which his promotion to the main team was announced, which, paradoxically, had lagged just behind the secondary.

Already at Red Bull, Vettel helped dispel all doubts about the team's bad previous campaign and helped secure the runner-up for the main energy drink team. The following year in 2010 Red Bull already achieved the constructors' title, which would be repeated until 2013 in a perfect alliance with Vettel. In 2014 Red Bull was overtaken by Mercedes, so Sebastian decided to sign for Ferrari, which was fourth behind Red Bull, Mercedes and Williams.

Vettel's first year at Ferrari ended with a constructors' runner-up, and the next he dropped to third place. In 2017, 2018 and 2019 he recovered and repeated the runner-up (always in the shadow of Mercedes), while 2020 was a fateful year that ended with Ferrari in sixth position.

Vettel therefore improved the situation of Toro Rosso and helped to achieve the best time of Red Bull. In Ferrari he achieved everything that could be achieved, uplifting the Italian team and keeping it in the runner-up against an unbeatable Mercedes (if we don't count the disaster of 2020). Faced with the only blemish in his history of not being able to help Ferrari fight against German hegemony, and counting on the final decline in his time as a Ferrari driver, his score is 8/10.

Soymotor.com

LEWIS HAMILTON

Lewis Hamilton joined the McLaren team when it had been third the previous season, far behind Ferrari and Renault in points... and helped the British team regain the championship (which would eventually be annulled in 2007). In 2008 McLaren obtained the runner-up to descend to third place in 2009. Between 2010 and 2012 he would continue alternating second and third places, after which, in a risky bet and with a visionary aptitude, Hamilton decided to sign for Mercedes, which was at that time fifth in the standings.

Hamilton's first year with Mercedes helped the German team rise to runner-up. And from 2014 to 2020, the story is already well known: Mercedes 'absolute dominance with seven consecutive constructors' titles.

Hamilton helped McLaren regain a title that would not materialize, although he was not able to achieve it legally after the suspension, but he did help keep the British team at the top of the standings. But after his jump to Mercedes, a team that by then was not positioned among the best teams, was key in the evolution of the German team and helped create the most dominating stage of Formula 1. A good performance in McLaren and an outstanding vision and support in his time at Mercedes give him a score of 9/10.

20minutos.es

FINAL CLASSIFICATION

Points Britos	lost Team	born		improve car		Years	Time 1° World	# WC	Brit
9		1911	1°	Fangio 10	65	21	2°	5	4
8	9	1969	2°	Schumacher 9	59	6	3°	7	2
9	8	1939	3°	Stewart 7	58	22	5°	3	2
6	8	1985	4°	Hamilton 9	58	8	2°	6	1
7	9	1936	5°	Clark 8	56	20	4°	2	1
10	9	1960	6°	Senna 9	54	13	5°	3	1
	8	1955	7°	Prost 8	52	14	6°	4	2
5	8	1987	8°	Vettel 8	52	8	3°	4	4
	9	1946	9°	Fittipaldi 6	48	20	3°	2	2
	6	1949	10°	Lauda 7	43	20	4°	3	2
	7	1981	11°	Alonso 5	38	7	4°	2	2
	4	1953	12°	Mansell 8	35	23	9°	1	1
9		1929	13°	Moss 10	31	19	—	—	—

CONCLUSION

Through this study, it is obtained that the best Formula 1 driver of all time is Juan Manuel Fangio. This would be consistent with other similar studies carried out by specialized media such as Autosprint or the University of Sheffield. And it is that it really does not take a great analysis to conclude that the Argentine is probably the best driver in history, with five world championships with different vehicles in a time without driving aids where the man mattered more than the machine.

But it is surprising, for example, to see Senna in sixth place. For many, he is the best Formula 1 driver of all time. Many people think that nobody has been able to drive a car like he did, with his temperament and hands that dominated the wheel like no other.

However, "driving style" is a difficult parameter to assess. And it may not even have a direct impact on performance and results. In this analysis we have tried to analyze objective factors (as far as possible). Aspects that could be compared with each other with figures or a high degree of objectivity. And even so, many of them have to be interpreted to give a final assessment. This is why Autosprint, for example, doesn't even include Senna in its top 10 drivers, and the University of Sheffield ranks him fifth.

This means that the result, in the end, will always depend on the factors analyzed. And of the importance that is given to each one. Surely you would have added some more, or eliminated others. Or you would have scored them differently.

With total security, in your mind you have a different final classification. And none is more correct than the other. Because it was already warned at the beginning: we are facing an impossible question. Who is the best Formula 1 driver of all time? It depends on what each one considers that a pilot has to have to be called that. Perhaps the question should be: what makes someone a better driver than the rest?

Each person will think that some qualities are more important than others. And some of them are not even measurable. That is the beauty of this matter, and of Formula 1 in general. The debate will be eternal, it will go beyond the competition itself. There will be as many rankings on the best driver of all time as there will be fans. And we will enjoy all of them, each one will have its essence, we will learn from these debates, even if in the end we do not get the answer we are looking for.

What I do hope, from the heart, is that this bet has helped you to get to know a little better these ten great drivers who could be at the top of many of these classifications. I hope you have enjoyed these pages, that this journey through the youth, trajectory and curiosities of each of these heroes has been useful to you, and that it has allowed you to discover unknown details and bring back fond memories.

If these pages trying to solve an impossible debate have made you enjoy them, then the objective is more than fulfilled, which is none other than to share this wonderful passion that is the maximum automobile competition.

Thank you very much for having trusted in this work, and for having shared what makes all fans connected in some way: the history of Formula 1.

THANKS

To all of you who at some point in my life have connected with me and I with you through motorsport.

To all of you who make Formula 1 more than just a sport.

To all those who have helped me with this work, and to those who will continue to do so, appreciating any possible incorrectness.

To all the media whose graphic resources have been referred to in this work, for making it showy.

Many thanks.
Jaren Cowan.

Printed in Great Britain
by Amazon